Sourcing Power

~ Source Wholesale Products ~

~ Sell Them For a Profit~

~ Build a Thriving,
Work-From-Home Business~

Nancy Alexander &
Jason Miles
With Jim Cockrum

should confer with a professional where suitable. Neither the publisher nor the author shall be responsible for any loss of profit or any other commercial injuries, including but not limited to special, incidental, significant, or other damages.

As of the writing of this book, all information is contained within is current.

TABLE OF CONTENTS

ABOUT THE AUTHOR

Nancy Alexander loves being a wife, mother, Mimi, sister, best friend, child of God, and Internet success story.

As a dreamer, artisan, teacher, public speaker, published author, coach, and Internet entrepreneur, it didn't take long for her to become known as a world-renowned floral and interior designer.

Those experiences equipped and molded her to take the world of sourcing by storm, which has only made her more successful at selling online.

Ladybug Wreaths, one of her many online businesses, was born after many years of running a storefront business. LadybugWreaths.com is now the hub of many of Nancy's online ventures.

Nancy encourages and trains students through her online community, BestOfNancy.com. She also sells her favorite floral supplies through her popular Amazon store, LadybugCertified.com. These supplies are available to Nancy through long-term relationships she developed with wholesale suppliers throughout the United States. How to find and build these profitable relationships is what Nancy wants you to take away from information you gain in this book.

Nancy and her family now have three websites and three Amazon stores located in the U.S. in the Fulfilled by Amazon (FBA) program, as well as one in the United Kingdom selling to European countries. —We are going global, Nancy says, —Amazon.ca (Canada)—You will be next!

The 35 years Nancy spent dealing with wholesale vendors at the largest national markets in the world, temporaries, and trade shows have really paid off. They have given her invaluable experience as well as the confidence she now uses daily to interact with established vendors and set up accounts with new vendors. These relationships are a vital part of sourcing new and profitable merchandise to sell online as well as in her family's several businesses.

Through this experience, Nancy felt well prepared to write this book. To be able to keep others from making the many mistakes she has made is what it is all about. I had to learn the hard way, but I want you to learn the easy way from an experienced veteran! Nancy says.

Nancy's patience and meticulous attention to detail has served to make her a very successful teacher and coach for her wreath-making students. That caring attitude and the drive to share her knowledge will make her indispensable to others who are just developing their own web-based businesses. She loves all of her students and shares in their joy and excitement with each and every accomplishment!

Nancy's dreams are to make YOUR dreams come true by teaching and equipping YOU to become a success through many different business models! You'll quite often hear Nancy's encouraging words: "You can do it; I know you can!"

I can do all things through Him who strengthens me.
- Philippians 4:13 -

Nancy's story, *"Fibromyalgia: Rumors, Ravages, and the Rescue"*, is in its finishing stages and should be released shortly.

Nancy is thrilled that Jason Miles has agreed to join her in the writing of this book. Jason is well known through many of his published —Power books such as: *Pinterest Power, eBay Auction Power, Instagram Power, YouTube Marketing Power,* and many more.

In addition to Jason, Nancy is blessed to also know, work, and partner with many of the most talented Internet Entrepreneurs in the business. Nancy has often been encouraged and coached by her mentor and dear friend of many years, Jim Cockrum.

Nancy admires Jim and calls him one of the most moral and ethical Internet marketers around, and all the while, Jim says, "Nancy has inspired *me* more than I could *ever* inspire her.

As a matter of fact, Jim has included Nancy in his bestselling book, _Free Marketing: 101 Low and No-Cost Ways to Grow Your Business, Online and Off._ This book is **THE number one** book on Internet marketing in the world!

Jim has changed the lives of Nancy and her family with his Proven Amazon Course. This course has honed their online selling skills by teaching them different methods of selling to develop various income streams.

It has taught Nancy, her husband Steve, and their son Andy that selling on Amazon and other online venues can be **very** profitable. This happened at a time when the company Andy managed went out of business, leaving him with nothing after investing fifteen years of his life there.

So, the four Alexanders (Andy, Stephanie, Steve, and Nancy) jumped into a brand-new Amazon business with Jim Cockrum's Proven Amazon Course.

Steve and Nancy had been sharing with Andy and Stephanie the many success stories contained in the Proven Amazon Course, and he was now ready to do whatever he could to bring in income for his family.

Even though Andy now has a new, well-paying job, he will never regret that life-changing move financially. And, he will never stop working on his profitable Amazon business, which continues to grow every day.

His goal is to continue building up his online sourcing-to-sell FBA business, and one day retire early enjoying being a stay-at-home dad and husband!

Sure, they had been a little skeptical at first, but who wouldn't be? Nancy was doubtful when she started her first online business many, many years ago, but her determination and hard work always paid off. This could be done again with Jim's new business model. Andy had a family to support, and the Alexanders were not afraid of hard work.

They were all ready to offer help to Andy so he could build a business of his own. He needed to support his family and give them a new start.

Nancy had already listened to Jim Cockrum's suggestions and encouragement as she developed many streams of income, as his _Silent Sales Machine_ book suggested. She acted on that advice in developing several online businesses that quickly became quite successful.

But, with Jim Cockrum's —Proven Amazon Course, the Alexanders are thrilled to say: Our family changed, our business changed, and our income definitely changed for the better. We learned that one of the most amazing online selling opportunities was right in front of us— Amazon! And, as of the writing of this book, we are going global with the help of Barrington McIntosh's "International Coaching" course.

ACKNOWLEDEGMENTS

This project has been a very special one for me. I have been blessed to have been mentored by Jim Cockrum, as I previously mentioned. I know that my business would not be where it is today, and I would not experience the joys of helping others, without Jim's encouragement and support. I will be forever grateful that God led our lives to cross over 10 years ago!

My husband Steve has been and will always be my GREATEST supporter and encourager! He is the love of my life and thinks I am the strongest, most courageous and brilliant person he has ever known. (I'm not so sure about that last one...) He is an engineer and project manager with Duke Energy, as well as a singer with his own band. But Steve also has a softer side as a writer, author, and poet. He is what you might call a —wordsmith, as he knows just the right word to help me express my thoughts at any given time.

**For I know the plans I have for you,
declares the Lord, plans to prosper you
and not to harm you,
plans to give you hope and a future.
- Jeremiah 29:11 -**

It has been such an honor to work with Jason Miles—a well-known, published author in his own right—as co-author of this book. To be able to work and publish with someone of his caliber is awesome.

We are so blessed to have been able to get to know Jason and his wife Cinnamon through Jim Cockrum's Mastermind group. Jason's knowledge about growing and managing an amazing business is truly a gift. His business, planning skills and writing skills as a published author have made such a difference in this book we are sharing with you today.

Have you heard the story of David Green?

The reason I ask is because, in my opinion, it's a story that every aspiring entrepreneur should hear, and as it happens, it contains several lessons directly related to this book. I think it will serve as a great introduction for us.

Let me tell you his story briefly, and then I'll explain the important principle it contains related to sourcing products.

In 1970, David borrowed $600 so he could start making miniature picture frames. Yep, picture frames. He cleared out his garage and started his new venture with high hopes. David didn't have a manufacturing system, so he employed his two sons, then nine and seven, and paid them seven cents for each picture frame they completed.

Two years later, in 1972, he took a big leap forward and expanded the scope of his operation to include a small storefront, just 600 square feet. They used the front 300 feet for the retail space and the back 300 feet to assemble the picture frames.

In an interview David said, "My wife worked the first five years for no pay... We just tried to put everything back in [the?] business."

Fast-forward to 2013, and David now has 578 stores

across the country, with more than 23,000 employees. His business opens 30 to 35 new stores each year. He sells over 65,000 items, including arts and craft supplies, furniture, fashion fabrics, baskets, silk flowers, and party supplies.

David's sales at the end of fiscal year 2012 were over 3.3 billion dollars. He has a personal net worth of over 5 billion dollars and is included on the *Forbes* list of American billionaires. David is a devoted Christian, and he donates half of his pre-tax earnings to Christian ministries.

By now, you've probably guessed that David's store is Hobby Lobby, the ultra-successful retail giant.

Stories like his inspire and amaze me for a couple of reasons. First, I can relate to the beginning—we still run our small business, Liberty Jane Clothing, out of our house. Second, I have hopes of one day relating to the ending—I wouldn't mind being a billionaire. Third, I admire his strong values and the way he expresses his commitment to his faith by giving a TON of money to charities.

So how does this relate to this book, to us, and to the topic of product sourcing? Let me outline a few key concepts that I hope you'll think about as you study this book and begin your product-sourcing journey.

1. How did David "scale up" from the single product to the 65,000 he now currently sells?

2. How did he "scale up" customers and go from

that first sale to 3.3 billion dollars in sales today?

David shares the answers to these questions in various interviews and in his book, *More Than a Hobby*. Let me share some of the insights that directly apply to aspiring entrepreneurs.

A Solid First Product

David started his business by creating his own version of a popular product. David had managed a five-and-dime store right after high school and knew that miniature picture frames were trendy. He set out to create a product that he could sell effectively.

Today, Hobby Lobby still makes many of its own products. The company has over 600 employees in its manufacturing department, where they make their own candles and fixtures.

Brand-Builder

David channeled his product into his own retail shop. The brand was "Hobby Lobby," and although it started small with just a 300-square- foot storefront, he focused on refining and strengthening it over time.

David installed strong brand attributes into the Hobby Lobby name, attributes directly linked to his personality and his family's values.

Today, Hobby Lobby is closed on Sundays, takes out giant ads on Christmas and Easter telling the Gospel story, and took the Federal Government to court over the Obamacare requirements.

You may personally hate all of these brand attributes, or you might love them. But no one can argue that they aren't very prominent aspects of the Hobby Lobby brand. David knew that in the heartland of America, those values would resonate with many customers. His boldness is a brand distinctive that has powerful influence.

Distribution Focused

David wasn't just building a brand, of course; he was building a retail strategy. When he is asked about his early days, he always says, —I love retail. That was his passion. He started small and grew his retail channel, adding one store after another. By 1985, 15 years after he had started, he owned 11 stores.

David knew that although he could make as many pictures frames as he wanted, he wouldn't grow a business if he didn't have a sales channel.

He focused on creating and growing retail stores.

In marketing terms, where you sell your product is called your "placement" strategy. He had a good place to sell his picture frames, and over the years, he grew that distribution channel to a national level.

Growth-Focused

David said in an interview recently, "We tried to do three things with cash: pay tithes, grow, and pay debt. We needed to balance these three things."

Hobby Lobby wasn't always debt-free, and David learned the hard way in 1985 that debt can really hurt you. He had banks threatening to liquidate Hobby Lobby's assets and power companies coming into the stores and turning off the power because they hadn't paid the bill. But they battled through those hard times and focused on paying off debt.

Today, Hobby Lobby is growing from earnings and opening 30 to 35 new stores each year without debt.

Generous

From the very beginning, David focused on generosity. In his case, this was tied to his personal religious values.

Today, Hobby Lobby gives away billions of dollars to charities each year. The company also focuses on ensuring that its employees are well cared for by providing a minimum wage of $13 an hour to full-time employees.

So How Does This Relate to Aspiring Entrepreneurs?

David's story is a textbook case of an entrepreneur focusing on the five key elements of building a company. You may have heard them before, but hopefully a quick review will be instructive.

Brand: Entrepreneurs focus on building a brand that customers love. Ideally, it will appeal to a core audience, have a memorable name, and have clear attributes or characteristics that help it stand apart from the competition.

Product: Entrepreneurs know that a good business grows out of sales of a good product. The better the product, the more likely it is that the business is going to flourish. Some entrepreneurs are product-makers and build a business as a way to sell their products. Some entrepreneurs start with a core audience and work to figure out which

products are a good fit for that audience. Eventually, if an entrepreneur is successful, she'll find a way to successfully serve a core audience with in-demand products.

Price: Your pricing strategy is one of the most important brand attributes you can orchestrate. Over time, you'll become known to your customers as a low-cost leader, a mid-tier competitor, or an ultra-premium provider. The most common strategies are the low-cost leader or the premium provider.

The most interesting fourth option related to online digital products is becoming known as the —free‖ provider. In that situation, you make your money via another method, such as advertising.

Placement: Where you sell your product is referred to as the placement or distribution strategy. Successful entrepreneurs find a good place, either online or offline, to find and sell to customers. Online services have sprung up to help, including Amazon, eBay, Etsy, Craigslist, and many, many more.

Promotion: Successful entrepreneurs find a way to promote their products, brands, and even themselves. They have three broad choices:

Paid Promotions – This includes paid advertising either online or offline.

Earned Promotions – This includes PR and media coverage for your product or brand. When you get in *USA Today* or on Oprah, you are benefiting from earned promotional help. Some brands are terrific at getting free publicity, and that helps them grow tremendously.

Owned Promotions – Over time, you acquire assets that help you promote yourself without needing to pay for it or —get lucky. The most powerful tool in this category is email marketing. Imagine launching a new product and having an email list of a million people to send the information to—wow, talk about a powerful selling tool. Other owned promotional assets include your website, your physical location and its signage, and any social media accounts you might have.

How to Apply These Lessons

So you might be thinking: *This is all very interesting, but what exactly do I do next?* Here is my very best recommendation for people who are starting at the very beginning.

Step One: Begin brainstorming a business concept you could create that would be focused on a very specific target market. Think narrow rather than broad.

For example, as you know from the introduction, Nancy's business is focused on wreaths, and my business is focused on doll clothes. Start with your passion for a topic and explore the options related to it.

Step Two: Read the information Nancy has written in this book and begin to explore sourcing options in support of your new business. Plan to visit a gift market and learn about the products that currently exist in your niche. Look online at the common sales locations, including Amazon, Etsy, eBay, and Craigslist, to see what is commonly available.

You'll frequently hear business advice that goes something like this: Look for a hole in the marketplace and fill it. For a beginner, that is terrible advice. Why?

When you are new to the industry, you don't understand what the customer wants or doesn't want. You don't have any idea what has been tried before. So, rather than going in arrogantly and assuming a lot about what the customer needs, go in cautiously and offer customers items that you know are already in high demand.

Step Three: Now that you've got a target market and a product to offer them, actually try to start selling it on eBay, Amazon, Etsy, or related sites. Don't —hypothetically do this step by asking your friends if they'll buy your product from you? They'll always say yes. Instead, actually try to sell the product. Build up your selling skills, a customer list, and a reputation.

One caution—in terms of getting inventory, be very frugal and careful. Don't assume that you will be successful in selling everything you buy. In fact, assume that you'll fail and that it will take longer than you expected. Therefore, don't purchase or pre-order much inventory at all, and certainly don't use credit. Start as small as you possibly can, because if you fail, you'll need to start over with another product and the money you've invested in the first product will be wasted. That's okay if it was a small amount. It's a nightmare if it was a large amount. So ignore the volume discount sales pitch at this stage. Remember, you're only testing.

It's at this critical step that you'll learn a ton of lessons about your product, your sales and marketing skills, your target market, and your competition.

You might find that your product is a horrible idea, when you had planned on it being a terrific idea. You might find that you have to dump the product and find another one. You might find that you have to dump the niche (target market) and find another one, because lots of niches are just plain bad for business. You might realize that you don't know anything about selling and need to go find a business partner who does or get additional training yourself. Remember the immortal words of Nietzsche:

"The doer alone learneth."

This proves it will work stage can take months or even years. That's fine. Sometimes, there are just no short cuts. That's perfectly okay as long as you keep working at it and moving forward.

Step Four: After you've found a product that works nicely, a way to identify and sell to prospects, and a marketplace that accepts you as a viable seller, there is only one thing left to do. Scale up your efforts.

You scale up by offering your product to an ever-widening audience via new distribution channels, and by offering your ever-widening audience more products that they need or want.

In short, you become the most complete provider in your niche.

Many entrepreneurs will plateau at a certain level of sales volume because they decide they don't want to grow any bigger, or they don't know how to grow any bigger. They might want to stick with just one product, or maybe they want to stick with just one distribution channel (such as eBay).

Growing bigger means tackling bigger problems and overcoming bigger obstacles. Ultimately, the size and scope of the operation will be a result of the skill of the operator, the strength of the brand, and the longevity and quality of the market niche.

Step Five: My fifth step is one you can ignore if you want, but I think it's important. After you've scaled your business up to a significant level, you should consider how to give back. Being generous is a bigger rush than almost anything else in life. Of course, David Green would argue that you should figure out how to give back from day one—from your first sale. I'm sure he's right.

Final Thoughts

This book is designed to help you overcome a very specific challenge how to professionally source products from gift markets and related locations. It is not intended to be a comprehensive business book. If you want more information about how to scale up your business, feel free to visit my blog, www.makesellgrow.com, or pick up some of my books at www.amazon.com/author/jasonmiles.

Jason G. Miles Seattle, WA

LET'S TALK ABOUT GIFT MARKETS AND TEMPORARIES

The largest gift market in the world is in Atlanta, Georgia. It used to be known as The Gift Market, but is now known as AmericasMart.

When major shows are held in Atlanta, there are also temporaries set up for a portion (approximately five days) of the show. These temporaries are exactly the same as a trade show, having a representation of many different products from many different vendors.

The largest trade show in the world is known as ASD. Hosted in Las Vegas, this massive show is essentially seven shows in one!

Going to a major market such as AmericasMart in Atlanta, Georgia is an experience unmatched by any other! I live closest to this market and have visited there numerous times. Attending a market is essential to a business owner, whether you have a storefront business or you sell online.

If you own a business or aspire to start your own business, you certainly must attend a major show at least once. It can revolutionize your business and open up a world of opportunity that will take your business to the next level.

With my help, you will gain so much knowledge about attending trade shows or major markets that you'll be amazed at how much your business will grow! You are opening up a whole new world of opportunity in your business. With your heightened business sense, you will be smarter placing orders with the vendors you meet and interact with at market.

What types of businesses am I talking about?

- Web-based businesses

- Selling on your own website

- International or global businesses

- Selling on Amazon, eBay, etc.

- Storefront businesses in your hometown

Choosing the wrong suppliers is costly in so many ways. First, you are not going to be happy with their service and certainly not with the problems they create. You are going to have to be on the phone a lot with them. You will be overcharged for their goods. Then, it's likely that their quality is going to be shoddy.

That creates severe (and sometimes lasting) problems with your customers, when they find that the goods they buy from you don't hold up. We haven't even addressed the time... hours, days; even months you will spend dealing with an unscrupulous supplier.

You could have been saving time, money, and effort using a fantastic supplier; instead you were dealing with your worst nightmare. All the while, your competitor enjoys an amazing advantage dealing with the competent rep you could have had.

Each trade show or market has different dates set up throughout the year. In general, each trade show and market has at least one major show per year that I find is crucial to attend.

The smaller ones throughout the year are still worth your time, but may not be as beneficial as the major ones. It is so important to do your research long before you plan on attending a trade show. This way, you can use your time and money wisely by attending the right trade show for you. Don't worry; I can help you decide which shows you should attend.

In Atlanta, the major gift and apparel shows usually last 10 days, so that two weekends are included. In my experience, the largest one is held in January every year. I purposefully attended this show in January because I didn't want to miss out on any of the new products my vendors were selling. By June, they often sold out of products I wanted to order!

NOTE: This supply and demand does vary from market to market, as do the hours of operation, so be sure to check with the one you plan to visit before you begin your trip.

In the **RESOURCE** section of this book, you'll receive facts about the major markets and trade shows, so you'll have all the information at your fingertips.

Just remember that you need to check dates, times, and locations each year, because these will and do change.

AMERICASMART ATLANTA

www.americasmart.com

Mission/Background: It is the nation's leading gift, home furnishings, and area rug marketplace and the largest trade mart/trade show complex of its kind in the world. More retailers from more places do business here than in any other U.S. wholesale market.

When: Twenty-three wholesale markets are hosted annually; six are dedicated to the gift and home furnishings markets. With the exception of AmericasMart's Florida gift & home furnishings market, all of the shows are held in Atlanta at the AmericasMart Atlanta campus.

Registration: AmericasMart is open to the trade only, and there is no fee to attend.

Sponsors: All of the markets are sponsored by AMC, Inc., the parent company of AmericasMart Atlanta.

Attendance: More than half a million people attend annually.

Target Markets: All retailers, from small specialty stores to large department stores and online sellers, are encouraged to attend.

Geographical Region of Attendees: Global reach — 50 states and

80 countries.

Dedicated Floor Space: 7 million square feet

Show Vendors: Diverse group of exhibitors spanning the gift, home furnishings, and area rug landscape. AmericasMart ensures that retailers have immediate access to the nation's largest single collection of products in categories including: garden, tabletop, fine linens and home décor, gourmet, holiday/floral, area rugs, general gifts, apparel, gift and resort, fashion accessories and fine jewelry, furniture and furnishings, etc.

Buying or Perusing: Buying retailers identify this show as the wholesale marketplace most important to their businesses.

Educational Sessions: The Discovery Series offers market attendees an extensive menu of practical, yet consistently modern and insightful, seminars. Topics range from business fundamentals and the bottom- line, to consumer behavior and trends, interior design, and design ideologies. Speakers are renowned industry professionals/experts.

floor
4
bridge level

Building ⊿

gift & home furnishings temporaries

Body & Soul, Boutique, Jewelry & Fashion Accessories, Down to Business,
Write C In! featuring Stationery & Scrapbooking

Open Friday, January 9
Tuesday, January 13
Closes at 5pm on Tuesday

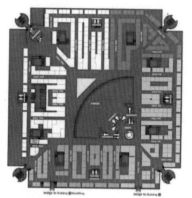

gift & home furnishings temporaries

Building ⊿

floor
4
bridge level

Body & Soul, Boutique, Jewelry & Fashion Accessories, Down to Business,
Write C In! featuring Stationery & Scrapbooking

Open Friday, January 9
Tuesday, January 13
Closes at 5pm on Tuesday

This exhibitor listing is based on confirmed participants as of November 14, 2008.
For additional exhibitor names and booth numbers, please refer to the supplement in this guide.

DETAILS & FACTS ABOUT AMERICASMART

I will be using AmericasMart as an example of how to register, what to expect, and a little about the experience, because it is the largest market in the world. But, at the end of this book, I am enclosing a list of other markets that all have similar qualifications as to how to register and shop with them.

More than 548,000 people attend AmericasMart annually!

AmericasMart Atlanta is the nation's only global wholesale marketplace housing the world's single largest collection of home, gift, area rug, and apparel merchandise.

Located in downtown Atlanta, the AmericasMart complex contains more than **seven million square feet of space**. Here is where manufacturers, designers, and sales representatives unveil and launch new designs and introduce new products.

AmericasMart in Atlanta is open year-round, Monday through Friday, from 10 a.m. – 4 p.m., with extended hours during special shows. It is closed to the general public. Visitors to AmericasMart must be active members of the retail or wholesale industry and be affiliated with a business that resells products represented in the venue's buildings.

Business credentials must be presented for entrance into any of the buildings.

AmericasMart temporaries offer more products in one place than anywhere else. Buyers can find the next new products from established favorites and fresh newcomers. With 34 categories, there's a specially designated temporary collection with innovative, creative options for any retailer.

This picture was taken at the apparel mart. There are floors for clothing, accessories, and shoes, plus many other floors housing a host of jewelry wholesalers.

I loved taking a quick break and shifting my mind to these products, since I always purchased a little something special for me!

Registration:

You can register online, or register by calling this number:

844-804-9444

The information below is copied from the AmericasMart website: To Become a Registered Buyer:

1. Read and review our New Buyer Admission Policies.

2. Fill out and submit the online pre-qualification form.

3. Submit your business credentials via fax (678-686-5302) or mail.

4. Receive an email confirmation of approval of credentials.

5. The first time you visit AmericasMart; remember to bring your photo identification (Driver's License or Passport) and a personalized business card.

Additional Buyers: To register additional buyers, they will need photo identification and either a business card with their name imprinted on it or a cancelled payroll check. This information can be faxed to 678-686- 5302, prior to attending, or it can be presented in person to the registration desk.

For More Information

Once you are approved as a new buyer, contact one of our Retail Services Representatives for personal information on shopping AmericasMart Atlanta. Please call 1-800-285-6278, extension 2461, to speak with a Retail Services Representative. We look forward to seeing you in Atlanta!

Advanced qualification expedites your entry into AmericasMart and is highly recommended. Qualified retailers who have previously attended an AmericasMart market are not required to register again.

Interior Designers/Architects/Landscape Architects **Please provide ALL of the following:**

- Professional membership card with recognized professional affiliation and valid government issued photo ID **OR** must qualify as a wholesale or retail business as provided above.

Guest Policy

- A limit of 2 guest badges per business, with a valid government issued photo ID.

- A cash-only, **non-refundable guest fee of $20** will be charged for all Gift & Home Furnishings, Rug, and Immediate Delivery shows.

Children Policy

- Children between the ages of 12 and 18 will be permitted admission as a guest with valid identification showing proof of age (i.e. birth certificate, school ID, passport, or other identification showing date of birth).

- Other than infants (as provided below) or child models credentialed by the Fashion Office and accompanied by an adult, children under 12 years of age are not admitted on showroom or exhibit hall floors for any reason. **No exceptions can be made.**

- Infants under the age of one year will be permitted admission as a guest if all of the below requirements are met:

  o The infant is accompanied by an adult at all times.

  o The infant is carried in a baby carrier or sling; **no strollers permitted**.

  o The parent or adult guardian signs a waiver and liability release.

- This policy applies to Buyers, Buyer Guests, Exhibitor Guests, and guests of AmericasMart personnel.

Take the following things with you, even if you have registered beforehand. You will be in a hurry, rushing to get in to start shopping. There will be many, many others there at the same time and as anxious as you.

- Photo ID – This can be your driver's license

- Picture of your business or a link to your website

- Photocopy of your business license (with your sales tax number on it)

- Voided business check with your business name and address

- Business card(s) with your name on it

- Other evidences that you are a legal business entity may be required

I also always took current pictures of the outside and inside of my business before going each time. Now that I have several websites, I make sure these website addresses are on my business cards.

Take a photocopy of your business license with your sales tax number on it. I always keep one of these on me at all times—I never know when I may need it. You may find a showroom that is selling samples, and vendors need a copy of this along with your number so they will not have to charge you sales tax.

A voided business check is a biggie. Now that I no longer have a storefront business in my hometown, I did not want to pay for a business account at my local bank. So, when we set up my new account, my bank suggested that I use all of the lines allowed to be printed on the check.

So, for instance, we put my name on the first line, my husband's name on the second line, and the name of my business on the third line.

Now, here is the trick: the bank considers the third line to be an address line. I only needed one line for my address, so the third line held my business name; the fourth, our address; and the fifth, our town, state, and zip code.

Business Cards

With all of the templates on Word these days, and with programs like Photoshop as well as online print shops, there is no excuse not to have a very professional-looking business card. I cannot stress this enough take lots of these with you!

The information on your business card is very important. On this card, I recommend:

- Your business name

- A tagline explaining what your business specializes in

- Your personal name listed as owner or proprietor

- The physical address of your business

At the bottom of the card, don't forget to put a website (or websites, if you have them) and a current phone number.

When designing my own business cards, I would change the tagline quite often. I do not want a tagline referring to floral supplies when I am sourcing other products to sell online. So, figure out different cards you might need and carry three or four along with you. So... easy!

You may want to receive a catalog from certain vendors, but they do not give out their expensively printed catalogs as freely as they used to. If you ask for one, chances are they will first ask for your business card, saying they will mail you one at the next printing. There are also some who do not give out catalogs unless you have just placed a reasonably large order.

Many vendors are now going to online shopping (via their own websites) for retailers. These sites are secure and are not open to the general public.

If you want access to their sites, make sure they give you log-in information showing prices, minimum orders, etc. before leaving.

Criteria from AmericasMart

In order to enter AmericasMart Atlanta, you must be associated with a business that resells products represented at this market. AmericasMart is very serious about what is required for wholesale and retail businesses. This means that you must have the following, as posted on AmericasMart website:

- Current retail business license

- Resale tax certificate

- Imprinted business check, credit card, or debit card

- Lease agreement for commercial space (for storefronts)

- Current invoice for bulk wholesale purchases (for online purchases)

NOTE: Sometimes, it is easy to get in with just a business check (your business name must be on it), a copy of your sales tax ID number, and a business card (which you can print yourself).

The list above is what is posted on the website, but I have found AmericasMart staff to be not quite as picky if you don't give them any reason to doubt that you are a reseller.

Don't forget; hold your head high! You have a right to be there just as much as everyone else you see milling around. And don't forget to make sure your business cards reflect that you are a reseller of the items you will be looking for at each particular show you are attending.

I have been known to attend markets/trade shows with several different cards in my possession. Each will pertain exactly to what I am interested in when talking with different wholesalers.

Internet businesses, take special note that you must provide proof of your operational e-commerce site!

You can bring two guests with you. Remember—children under 12 are not allowed.

If you are new to AmericasMart, it will help if you go online to pre- register as a registered buyer by filling out the proper forms and submitting your business credentials ahead of time. This will make your entry faster, and you will receive your badge when you arrive.

Check out the website for all the information and details, including information about lodging and the showrooms that will be open during your visit: www.americasmart.com/open-daily.

If you can't make it to one of the major gift shows at AmericasMart in Atlanta or one of the other major gift show locations, during the year, you can visit the permanent shops that stay open year-round on weekdays.

They are open Monday through Friday, with numerous gift, home, holiday, and floral showrooms open for you to leisurely explore. They also offer free parking during this time as an incentive for you to visit.

While it is nice that venues offer this opportunity to see showrooms throughout the week, I recommend that you plan accordingly and save your time and resources so you can attend one of their major markets throughout the year.

If you only visit during the week, you will miss out on the temporary businesses that are set up during market times, and you can potentially miss out on a lot of great deals.

Temporaries at AmericasMart are very similar to trade shows. They show most of the same merchandise and are widely attended!

MY PERSONAL EXPERIENCES AT AMERICASMART

While I owned a storefront business, "The Straw Basket", I made the trip to Atlanta each year in January, as well as several other times during the year. I normally stayed four to five days in January, as I ordered ahead for the entire year. Yes, even Christmas!

I'll never forget the first time I went to a national gift market.

It was 1989, and the market was held at AmericasMart (then known as the Atlanta Gift Market.)

I planned ahead, or so I thought. My plans included notes of products I wanted to search for, as well as vendors and wholesalers I wanted to meet and talk to. I also had lists of products I was already sure I wanted to place orders with. And yes, I did talk and plan extensively with someone experienced with the Atlanta Gift Market.

However, the trip was a total disaster and cost me tons of money!

I don't want this to happen to you! This was a new experience for me, and I did plan ahead. But still, the trip was a big expense.

Looking back, I just keep thinking: *What if I had not known the little I did know, and what if I was really unprepared?"*

I can't even let myself think about that one. And, if you are reading this book—Congratulations!—you don't have to worry about that either.

The January show in Atlanta is the largest one of the entire year. Retailers or resellers (meaning YOU) have just gone through their busiest selling season. Your bestselling products are fresh on your mind. In addition, you are also looking for the newest and best products being introduced at market for the coming year.

In January, the showrooms have been totally reconstructed to reflect spring, summer, and brand-new Christmas items... with samples. NOTE: Samples are an important part of the education we're sharing here. In fact, let's talk about that right now:

It is very important to take a moment to talk about the word "samples." All of the products you see in each showroom, temporary booth, or trade show, are not really in the vendors' possession yet—that is to say, unless they were left over from the previous spring, summer, or Christmas seasons.

*They have only received a sampling of some of the "test" products for the upcoming seasons. These wholesalers are like us: they **test first** before tying up thousands or hundreds of thousands of dollars of their funds in products while not knowing if they will become bestsellers. We'll discuss this more, but first let's get back to my first market experience...*

Reserve a room as close as you can to the market or trade show, if you are staying more than one day. Learn where the nice restaurants are, and treat yourself with a nice meal while relaxing after a long day.

Soon, you'll be returning to your room to begin going over your notes and looking at catalogs (if you were able to get any).

The first one or two days spent at markets and trade shows should be dedicated to covering as much territory as possible. We walked very quickly up and down long hallways lined with showroom after showroom, moving our heads back and forth as quickly as we could.

Yes, you do sometimes end up with a bad headache! Don't forget to bring whatever it is you take for a headache.

We then walked up and down many long aisles, with booths on each side, in the huge center where trade shows and temporaries were held. It is important to move very fast—you don't have time to waste!

At AmericasMart, we passed by many showrooms with only a quick glance. Others were more tempting, as I spied many interesting or newly introduced lines through their glass facades.

These demanded more attention as we entered, perused their wares, and asked for catalogs and business cards. It was also important to meet their contact personnel before leaving quickly with scribbled notes, if we were not ready to purchase yet.

If I were making a first visit today, I would definitely be carrying my small audio recorder. As I am walking, I can talk about interesting products and showrooms or mention a booth name, building floor, and/or room number.

The picture below was taken in the apparel mart. This is only one of the buildings you can visit while attending AmericasMart.

Actually, this is the one I liked best. I went here to unwind while looking at beautiful clothing and jewelry. Most of these showrooms sell samples, so I'm sure you can imagine that I had lots of fun here. Steve would always have to remind me that my time was up, and we needed to get back to work.

There was one firm rule I followed at each market and trade show if, and only if, I was going to be in attendance for more than one day...

ABSOLUTELY NO PURCHASES WERE TO BE MADE ON THE FIRST DAY!

There were way too many temptations as I walked up and down those long halls from showroom to showroom and booth to booth.

It was necessary that I spend my money wisely, so I strived to focus (with blinders on if necessary), and not spend my money because of the glitzy displays, bright lights, and appealing merchandise.

The trade show atmosphere is electric—energy is enticing!

It's like no place you've ever been before. It is so easy to get caught up in this new world of wholesale vendors and resellers, as deals are being made all around you.

Before you know it, buyer's fever has enticed you into spending way more than you planned. Fast talkers have your attention, enticing you to think you certainly can sell items you might reconsider, if you pulled back—alone—to really think.

On the second day, while we were still completing our walk-through, we decided that some items were just too good to pass up. The last day or days were the planned days spent ordering only. Of course, this plan is dependent on how many days you have to spend at the market or trade show.

The walk-through was hard; it was exhausting, especially with my own body being not quite up to par as I always wish it were. But I knew from my own experience that it was necessary in order to come home with products that would sell well and would become great income- producing finds.

I'll warn you—after a day at a market/trade show, your head will be spinning with ideas and products that you know you can make a profit on, and you'll be the most drained that you've ever been in your life.

I'm telling you this, because your brain will not be at its sharpest by this time, when you are making serious decisions.

After one or two days taking in as much as humanly possible, wouldn't you think it was time to crash? Well, you definitely want to and need to. But, I've got news for you that thought is wrong! Life-changing business decisions are still looming ahead, waiting to be made. Those decisions can make a difference in whether your business succeeds or fails.

Therefore, this is when the real work just begins.

I spread out catalogs collected during the day, along with many notes of great deals and favorite products. They were laid out on whatever flat surface was available. I had no computer in the early years, as I began the slow, tedious (but necessary) task of pouring through all of the important information and notes that I had collected.

Showrooms and booths had to be put into some sort of order. Then, products that I thought I could sell at a nice profit formed another list. I quickly discovered that many products I liked could be found at several different showrooms or booths. That is when I had to compare pricing, terms, and sales reps.

NOTE: This is where you could also try to find the real source of the product that you think would be a definite moneymaker for you. The more middlemen you can skip, the better off you'll be.

After this was done, I put together a map for the next day. Yes, we would be covering some of the same territory again, but this time, I knew where to stop and spend valuable time. And, now, I had an idea of what products I would purchase and how many of them were within my budget.

At the January show, retailers and wholesalers are just getting over the Christmas season. Although their showrooms or booths are spruced up with new products for the upcoming season, they are also still selling leftover Christmas items at greatly reduced prices.

Sometimes, this can be a really good source for you, but it can also break the bank. You might end up purchasing leftover goods you are sure you can sell, and then can't. Just remember this slippery slope.

They are leftover products, and can get you in trouble! Now, I know for many people who source to sell online, these deals may be great finds, but they also may not... just a note a caution here.

Everyone is looking for that new product, color, style, or design that will catch the eye of your customers—you know, that special something to entice customers to buy. You want to be the first to source and sell the newest product at the best price. This can be a daunting task and hard to accomplish... But, you can!

I thought that ordering in January assured me that I would receive exactly what I ordered. I had to learn the hard way by not receiving the items I really wanted. So, don't forget—the merchants or vendors are testing products, and if some products don't pass the test, you will not be receiving your shipment. Always be sure that you're aware of this when you order. I would guess that about 15 to 20 percent of my January orders never arrived.

INSIDER SECRETS REVEALED!

An interview with a 38-year veteran market and trade show rep reveals secrets and tips!

As I talked with John, a sales rep for many different wholesalers during his 38-year career, I told him how, many years ago, I was taken advantage of because I was new to purchasing wholesale products.

It is important for you to get insider information so you will not make the same mistakes I did. John has been my own sales rep for years, so I know he is trustworthy. We had a very informative conversation that I think will really benefit you.

Insider Tip: Sales reps can smell a newbie!

His first response when I told him I was —taken was: They all too frequently throw out some industry slang to see if the customer will pick up on it. John said that a rep can read it on your face if you don't know what you're talking about. This leads a rep to take advantage of you.

<u>Those are bad reps</u>.

How to dress at markets/trade shows:

Of course, wear tennis shoes, but don't dress up too much when attending markets and trade shows. *As a matter of fact, dress down a little.* Sales reps are smart.

They can see an expensive watch or an expensive handbag. They are very good at reading how much money you have to spend just from the way you dress! They pay very close attention to these signs, because they work on commission.

When walking through a market or a trade show, if you truly think a product will be a bestseller for you, leave your business card as you are getting the rep's name and phone number.

Sometimes, a busy show just isn't the place to get to know each other. You might make an appointment to meet for dinner or use Google Hangouts online. A more relaxed atmosphere is the best place to write an order. Most of them will still give you their show specials, even if you do not place an order right then.

Examples of show specials might be:

- Free shipping

- Percentage off your order, maybe 10%

- Larger discounts on certain items, depending on quantity

Catalogs are getting more expensive to print. Reps for companies are stingier about giving them out unless they know they are getting an order right then or making an appointment to write an order. If you place an order at the show, you will receive a catalog—that is, if the company still produces one.

Key Terms: Dating

Dating goes from charge card, to Net 30, Net 45, Net 60, Net 90, Net 120, Net Christmas or spring dating. Net Christmas or spring dating sometimes lasts as long as six months, depending on the showroom.

Insider Tip: Drink lots of water! Exhaustion catches up with you, making it hard to think.

Often, people forget to take their meds or don't hydrate, and John has seen people pass out. Some say it's worse than (or just as bad as) being in an airplane. All those bodies act like little heaters and warm up the spaces. This dries up the air.

If you are at a market, this is why you will notice that many of the rooms are extremely cold in the mornings, as they are trying to get a jump on all the body heat. Take a lightweight sweater that you can remove as the day warms up.

If you are staying overnight, take a cool mist humidifier for the hotel room to ward off sickness. It will keep you hydrated and refreshed for the next morning. You want to be sharp each day and full of energy.

Most importantly, take a business sheet (lots of them!).

Business sheets always include:

- Business name and links to websites

- All contact information

- Federal and state identification numbers

- How long you have been in business

When you are placing an order and filling out an application, you can save time by having all that information written down on one piece of paper.

A great tip from John: Often, after you place an order, your rep will ask you to take about 10 minutes to fill out an application. You don't have 10 minutes to spare at a market or trade show. This is so simple. You are now prepared! Hand them your business sheet, sign the application, and let the rep fill out all of the information for you.

Insider Tip: Always, always ask for a printed copy of the order.

Make sure it has the signature of the person who sold you the goods. Have him or her sign and date the order. Or, if your rep can't give you one on the spot, John says that many reps accommodate their customers by emailing the order to them before they leave the booth or showroom.

Check on your smartphone or iPad to make sure it is there. If reps will not do this for you, then you don't want to do business with them.

When attending markets or trade shows, as you gain experience, you will learn where the free drinks and the free food are located. But if it doesn't fit into your plan, don't go out of your way just to get a free breakfast! It could take up too much valuable time if you have to cross over into another building. Free isn't really free if it costs you valuable time.

Insider Tip: Sales reps don't care if you sell on Amazon or the Internet.

They need to know that the account is stable. Now, there could be a different opinion if you are talking to the owner of the company. They do not want to de-value their goods by having them sold online at a lower price than they might sell them in a retail setting.

There is nothing more aggravating to a sales rep than someone who comes in and says I'm thinking about opening a business, or I've been in business for two weeks. Don't say that to sales reps, or you won't get much of their time.

You can describe your business. For example, you can say I'm 60% online and I'm 40% pop-up shop. Pop-up shop is a new term for businesses that might sell at a fair or at smaller craft or trade shows.

As John reminds us, reps have to be very selective about how they spend their valuable trade show time too!

When buying in quantities, how much of a discount can someone expect?

Buyers need to know three terms:

1. Minimum order, minimum quantity

2. Case

3. Master case

Basically, these are like small, medium, and large.

- On average, you can expect a 5 to10 percent discount when buying a case pack.

- On a master case, you might receive as much as a 20 percent discount, but it all depends on the individual vendor.

- Some vendors have tiered pricing, meaning that they don't have cases or master cases. But if you spend a certain dollar amount, you can get a deeper discount. It's all determined by the quantity bought from that vendor.

Insider Tip: Beware of tiered pricing! Sometimes tiered pricing can blow your budget, because you spend extra just to get the discount, and you end up not being able to sell it all.

- The vendors will tempt you to you to buy more especially if they suspect you're a newbie.

- I got caught up in tiered pricing one year in a showroom that I had walked by many times before.

- I let them talk me into quantities that took me four to five years to finally move.

Insider Tip: Watch out for buyer's fever.

Some buyers get caught up in buyer's fever and come home with invoices totaling more than they can afford.

They get stuck with a massive amount of product they can't sell. These items then become outdated. It's much better to buy small amounts, testing your product to make sure it will sell before you purchase in volume.

If you have the resources to buy a huge lot of product and sit on it, still be careful, because your predictions can still be wrong.

Common Questions:

Which time of year is best to attend markets and trade shows?

If possible, always book Christmas items in January, never later than March! John agreed that if you wait until July, all you may find is spring products for the following year.

Be prepared that when you receive your order, you may be missing several pieces. The reps don't explain that what you see in the showroom is just a demo piece. Many times, that piece never goes through production, because there was not enough interest, or enough people didn't order it. That is just a downside to this business.

What about temporaries and trade shows? Are they the same, or different?

Trade shows and temporaries are exactly the same. You walk as fast as you can; your head is on a swivel. You do not stop unless you see something truly exceptional! When you do, and then stop.

- Have a short conversation.

- Exchange business cards.

- Write yourself a note on the back of the card (or a sticky note).

- Have a wallet or pouch just to accumulate these cards/notes.

- Sort through them when you return home and go through your notes.

If you are at a market, start on the top floor in the morning, so by the time you get to the temporaries on the bottom floor, the rush should be over, and it will be easier to get through.

Can you order in large quantities from temporaries?

Yes! You may find businesses that have been around a long time that have their own warehouses and showrooms elsewhere.

If you are at the market, you'll find them set up in temporaries. The exact same businesses sell at trade shows like The Associated Surplus Dealers (ASD) Show.

John says not to be afraid to carry on a conversation with anyone you are considering doing business with. Reps will certainly ask you many questions before selling to you!

Insider Tip: Interview vendors! You have the right to ask all about their business, too.

- What is your minimum opening order?

- What dating options do you offer?

- What is your re-order amount?

- Are you a single company, or do you represent many different businesses with different opening orders?

- How many customers do you have in the U.S.?

- Do you sell overseas?

- Do you have warehouses overseas, and where?

- How can I find out if you are selling to anyone else who is in my market area?

- How long have you been in business?

- Do you have referrals I can contact?

- Do you have these items in stock?

- What is your ship date?

Insider tip: Use common sense. The product may look great, but if the people are shady, RUN!

- If a deal looks too good to be true, then it probably is!

- There could be black market goods, or your order may never be filled, or it could be overly delayed.

- Stay focused. Don't be so overwhelmed at everything that is going on around you that you aren't paying attention.

Always ask to meet with your local rep, the one who actually lives in your territory.

Reps from other parts of the country may try to sell you everything in the showroom or booth just to get a good commission.

Many temporary reps are brought in for market shows as well as trade shows. They are there to put as much money in their pockets as they can in a short time.

NOTE: You can ALWAYS get a better deal with reps who live in your region. Like John, they want to take better care of you, because they are interested in building a relationship.

Trade shows and temporaries are practically the same thing. Look past the glitz and glamour to see the value.

DIFFERENCE BETWEEN A TRADE SHOW & MARKET

When AmericasMart hosts its popular shows for the year, you can also attend the temporaries. These are booths set up just like ASD and include many choices of products from vendors all over the world. The wide variety provides you additional options to find whatever you may be searching for.

When I first started attending this market, everything was located in one building. But this building was huge. It was 14 stories tall, and on each floor, there were anywhere from 30 to 60 showrooms, depending on the size of each showroom. So you could literally spend days in one building.

Now AmericasMart is located in four of the tallest buildings in the center of downtown Atlanta.

On every odd-numbered floor, there are covered walkways that cross the Atlanta streets below, taking you to another building. Cover that same floor before catching an escalator to start covering the next floor. These crosswalks give you more mobility and let you cover more showrooms and booths, while saving you time.

TRADE SHOWS FROM A VENDOR'S PERSPECTIVE

Trade shows and conferences have really become cottage industries. There are many smaller ones located in and around this great country. So, look for one close to you.

John says that vendors look forward to trade shows, markets, and conferences, because this gives them an opportunity to meet their prospective customers face to face as they discuss and show off their wares.

Vendors also love showing at the larger trade shows, because this gives them a chance to target A-level decision makers rather than B- or C- level decision makers.

The same goes for people attending trade shows, markets, and conferences. You definitely want to attend the shows where you have access to the A-level decision makers who have the authority to adjust pricing accordingly.

Vendors love events where they have access to names as well as email or mailing addresses of registered attendees.

John says that this gives them the opportunity to create that buy-and- sell relationship with you way before the show begins.

It is definitely costly for vendors to attend a big market or trade show. There are many expenses as they decide how to best showcase their products and provide signage and eye-catching displays.

Successful Selling

Vendors' success in convincing you to purchase depends on many things. First, how good are their products? And how well do their sales reps show and discuss these products?

It is of utmost importance that they understand their potential buyers. No good A-, B, or C-level decision makers are going to spend their time talking with someone whom they know from experience is not going to buy. They could easily get stuck with a big talker who walks away after an hour saying, "Well, I'll think about it and let you know."

So, vendors are knowledgeable and savvy, just as you need to be during the deal-making process.

Out of the corner of their eye, as they are talking with you, sales reps are trained to notice the many people who are wandering in and out of their booths.

The one person who walks away, because the owners and sales reps are tied up with others, could be the one who would have made a large enough purchase to make their entire trip and setup worthwhile.

Like John, if reps are really good at what they do, I guarantee you that they'll know exactly which ones are the potential purchasers, as well as the ones who are the talkers and browsers.

Show Promotions

These vendors often offer show promotions. Some of these transactions are really easy for you to close, and some are not. It is the vendors who make this a quick and easy transaction that are most likely to get the largest share of your business.

Vendors sometimes offer their purchasing customers bonus buys, which consist of items offered to you because you just placed a large order with them. For them, these extra-special bonuses and efforts really go a long way.

Business Networking

Vendors have gone to all the trouble to register, set up, and attend major trade shows and markets because they know the value of business networking.

You, too, are attending this same trade show or market to set up mutually beneficial relationships. *You both desire to increase business revenue or increase your bottom line.*

For a mutually beneficial agreement, vendors want to receive your business information, contact information, and get a feel of what product (or products) you might be interested in purchasing.

And, you, as the attendee, are just as interested in contact information and setting up mutually beneficial agreements, so that you will leave with a lead to products you can resell and bring in more income. You are both interested in growing your businesses. *Vendors are just as anxious as you to "seal the deal."*

"The problem is never how to get new, innovative thoughts into your mind, but how to get old ones out.

- Dee Hock, Founder of Visa -

PREPARATION TO ATTEND A SHOW

Let's talk about how to prepare for a major gift market or tradeshow.

Physical Preparations

After you register online, read through all of the promotional material. You might want to read through it several times to get a solid knowledge of the show you are attending!

Remember... *KNOWLEDGE IS POWER!*

Make a list of the must-see booths. These are the vendors that sell products that you are extremely interested in. This is a fluid list that may change as you plan, but it's important to get it down on paper, so you know where you are headed.

Study the map of the building so that you understand the locations of potential vendors on your list. Try to put them in order by location.

Next, make a list of booths that you want to see, but that aren't crucial to see. These vendors may sell products that you have an interest in, but may not be exactly what you need. If you aren't sure about them, write them down, and you can cross them off later if necessary.

The map will help you determine your route each day, so you aren't walking in circles or backtracking. Like I said earlier, these buildings are huge, and you will tire yourself out if you are aimlessly walking about!

ASD TRADE SHOW

The largest trade show in the U.S. is held in Las Vegas, Nevada. www.merchandisegroup.com

This show is held twice yearly, in March and August.

Registration: It is free to the trade. This show is not open to the public.

Sponsors: ASD/AMD's Las Vegas Gift Expo is produced by VNU Expositions' ASD/AMD Merchandise Group and runs in conjunction with the ASD/AMD Trade Show-Las Vegas and the ASD/AMD Jewelry Show at the Mirage, also in Las Vegas.

Attendance: In excess of 55,000.

Target Markets: Independent gift retailers, national chains, and buying consortiums.

Geographical Region of Attendees: National.

Dedicated Floor Space: 12,000 square feet solely dedicated to gift product channels.

Show Vendors: 500 companies exhibit in 1,200 booths, selling products in all gift and variety categories.

Buying or Perusing: It is primarily a buying show—no cash and carry—order writing only.

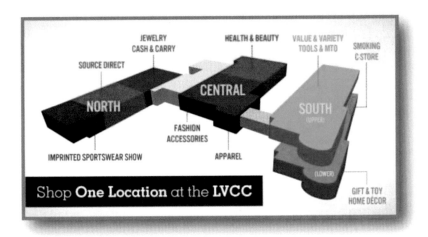

Shop **One Location** at the **LVCC**

Why attend the ASD trade show?

Attending an ASD trade show gives you direct access to manufacturers from around the world. SOURCEDIRECT at ASD offers importers, distributors, wholesalers, designers, and production professionals a dedicated sourcing show to meet face-to-face with contract manufacturers and factories from around the globe, saving them time and travel costs.

SOURCEDIRECT will offer more than 300 factories in the following popular categories:

- **Apparel & Footwear** – affordable footwear, fashion apparel, lingerie, fashion hosiery, resort wear, blanks, t-shirts, swim/cover-ups, work wear

- **Consumer Electronics** – cases, covers, ear buds, fans, headphones, PDAs, tablets, iPhone fashion accessories, speakers, watches

- **Fashion Accessories** – bangles, belts, bracelets, earrings, eyewear, furnishings, gloves, handbags, hats, headwear, jewelry, leather accessories, luggage, necklaces, scarves, tote bags, umbrellas

- **Gift & Handicrafts** – art, candles, clocks, crystal, decorations, figurines, gifts, gift bags, gift wrap, holidays, lighting, office accessories, party supplies, picture frames, special occasion, stationery, tchotchkes

- **Home & Garden** – bath, bedroom, ceramics, glassware, home décor, hard goods (pots/pans/utensils), home textiles, hospitality, linens, plastic goods, tabletop

- **Outdoor** – athletic accessories, balls, bats, boards, camping, caps, clubs, exercise, gloves, hike, sporting goods, tactical knives, shoes, uniforms

- **Style & Beauty** – cosmetics, color care, general beauty enhancement, hair, lips, lotions, skin care, nails

- **Toys** – games, novelty, plush, toys

- **Volume & Variety** – chain store, discount variety products, dollar store, promotional, seasonal

- **Miscellaneous** – adult novelties, energy drinks, accessories

Convenient, efficient, and productive, ASD is held two times a year in Las Vegas. You can get more done in less time at ASD.

There is no better place to source for new suppliers and products, work all your options, and make the best buying decisions for your business, with products conveniently merchandised by country and category.

Who attends ASD?

Import buyers with knowledge and experience with import regulations and logistics, international shipping, foreign wire transfers and production lead times. Over 15,000:

- Importers / distributors

- Wholesale companies

- National retail chains / mass merchants / chain stores

- Mail order catalogs

- Exporters

- ASD exhibitors buying groups

- Sourcing agents

Many top sourcing countries attend ASD.

- Bangladesh
- China
- India
- Korea
- Mexico
- Pakistan
- Taiwan
- Turkey
- Vietnam

This trade show is not open to the general public. You are required to show business identification and a government-issued photo ID to receive a badge and be allowed into the show.

If you select your business type as a retailer, you must be able to prove you are a retailer by presenting a retail business license and invoices showing purchases of finished goods in the last six months.

NOTE: A new password will be created for you at each show, and you do have to register for each event you attend separately. If you register ahead of time, there is no fee. However, if you wait until you are there to register, the fee is $30.

You can go to the ASD website's directory section to get a list of all the exhibitors. If you find that it is impossible for you to attend a show, you can click on each vendor name in the directory to receive all the contact information for that particular vendor.

Appointments! Appointments! Appointments!

Your time is valuable!

Find out if you can schedule an appointment with an exhibitor that you are very interested in seeing. This will save you time and frustration!

Don't waste your time standing around a showroom or booth hoping to speak with the owner if you can help it. Remember, you want to try and cluster your appointments so you save on walking.

Plan on bringing your tablet or iPad to jot down notes and links to vendor sites. You also can email yourself information that you don't want to forget when you get back home from your trip. A small device like a tablet will be much easier to carry versus a large laptop.

Speaking of technology and smartphones, do some research and find out if the trade show or market you are visiting has an app for your phone. It just might contain handy information for you, like a list of vendors and a map.

I always look up the item I am about to purchase with my iPad or iPhone. You can usually find out if the price you have been given leaves room for you to make a nice profit.

Years ago, we purchased a lightweight, rolling cart to carry catalogs collected during each day. Believe me; this one item has been worth much more than its purchase price!

It is much easier to pull those heavy catalogs than it is to carry them on your shoulder in a large bag. Speaking of shoulder bags, if you're a woman, leave it at home! Wear a fanny pack. Or, you can always bring your spouse or a friend with you.

It's worth saying again—wear comfortable shoes! Your feet will thank you later, I promise. Make sure your clothing is professional and neat. You want to feel comfortable and relaxed in order to keep up with the demands of the day, but don't look sloppy and unkempt.

You want to make a good first impression on potential vendors without showing off too much! Do dress down a little. Leave diamonds, expensive jewelry or watches, and expensive brand-name bags at home.

Prepare a written list of your social media facts that you can easily share with potential vendors. They want to know how many followers you have. Bring several copies of this list with you, so you won't run out.

Finally, don't forget to pack snacks. You will need the boost of energy in order to keep up with the physical demands of attending a trade show or market. Hydration is essential, so bring a water bottle. You will tire out faster if you aren't staying hydrated. Food purchased at markets and trade shows is VERY expensive.

Mental Preparations

Let's talk about building your confidence as a successful entrepreneur. Helen Keller once said, Never bend your head. Always hold it high.

Look the world straight in the face. What she was talking about here is confidence.

Be proud of yourself for taking action steps to grow your business by attending a trade show or major market. You are taking a huge step in the right direction, and it will pay off.

Spend some time reminiscing about a past success in your business, something that you feel really good about. It might be a wise decision regarding a big purchase that really paid off, or it might be some action you took with social media that increased your following. Whatever it might be, remember how powerful and confident you felt and use those strong emotions to bolster you as you prepare for this trip.

Here are some great tips to go over before you start negotiating in a busy showroom:

- Have a clear strategy in mind for your business needs.

- Remember to always stay calm.

- Do not let the overwhelm factor knock you off your game.

- Show respect to vendors, and remember that they are not obligated to give you an awesome deal.

- A friendly, calm discussion will always get you the best prices.

Body Language Is Critical

Yet, it is often overlooked as a part of your negotiating strategy. As you learn to control the nonverbal communications in your conversations with vendors, you will increase your likelihood of success.

Stay positive! You can do this! Don't start on your trip on the wrong foot with worries or fears. With strong preparation and a clear vision in mind, you will make successful business decisions that will have great outcomes.

When You Arrive

Follow the tips below to make things run smoothly:

- Consult the newest trade show directory to see if any vendors you want to see may have dropped out.

- Don't grab every catalog or brochure that's handed to you.

- If you're not interested in the material, politely decline and move on. Those catalogs will get heavy very quickly!

Ask if the vendor can mail a catalog to you, if it is one you might want to look at later and don't want to carry it around. Also exchange business cards—this is very important!

A Vendor's Booth

Quickly determine if the person you are talking with can help you with your specific needs. If he or she can't, politely ask to speak to a manager or owner. Don't waste your time (or their time) if they can't help you.

Pack your business cards (lots of them), but have your smartphone or tablet handy to send yourself information about what you've seen.

Allow time in your schedule to be open or free. You will be seeing lots of new products and ideas that you may not have planned for. So make sure you have time for those unexpected stops.

NEGOTIATING STRATEGIES

If you understand the rules of negotiating, you will walk away with better prices for products and future business arrangements.

You'll find that shopping at trade shows and markets provides you with hundreds of opportunities to learn about new products and find new vendors. But you'll be more successful in finding new products and setting up future business arrangements if you apply some simple techniques:

- Pay attention to and learn others' cultural practices.

- Understand that a firm handshake in our country may mean that the deal is sealed, but in other countries, it may only mean that you have done some negotiating, but there is more you need to address.

- Show respect to the person you want to strike a deal with.

- There is a way to negotiate with a smile on your face but with a firm demeanor.

- I do this same type negotiating at yard sales, with a smile, a little hesitation, and a twinkle in my eye.

- I did this for years when attending shows, so it becomes second nature to me now. I am comfortable with it. You can be, too!

Always listen and let the other people finish their sentence or thought before you come back with a counter offer. You have to be polite, firm, and honest.

If the vendor does not seem to like your offer, and if you think his price is too high, be prepared to walk away. You are not obligated in any way if you have done your best in this process to find a moneymaker for your own business. Believe me, there are plenty more opportunities right around the corner.

Even if you're not sure you can end up making a deal that is profitable to you, it is nice to be helpful when talking with people to offer your services, or at least your suggestions, as to how to improve on and market their business.

Do this with no expectations, except that you are sincerely interested in helping them succeed. Vendors do not know you. They don't know if you are a good person and an honest person who stands behind his or her word.

Offering assistance proves that you are sincere, helpful, and interested in their business. It may also indicate that you are probably honest.

Wouldn't you rather do business with a person whom you know is trustworthy? Well, your vendor would also!

SOME SUPPLIERS PREY ON NAÏVE NEWCOMERS

I want to point out upfront that what I'm about to say is certainly not always the case. Many, many vendors I have worked with are amazing people who are sincerely interested in my success. Why shouldn't they be? After all, when I am successful in selling their products, I will definitely come back to purchase more and more items from them.

But, I'm sorry to say, there are also some vendors who prey on you because of your timid approach to purchasing, born out of your ignorance or just the fact that you are a newbie to the entire market/trade show process.

They quickly discern that you are not prepared with good questions and are vulnerable to being taken advantage of.

They actually use your eagerness to turn the business against you, loading you up with out-of-date, non-selling merchandise while trying to convince you what a great deal you are getting.

And without competitive pricing on the best materials for your business, you really have **NO chance—I repeat, NO chance—of succeeding.**

I have been in this business in both retail (storefront) and Internet situations for almost 35 years now.

I had to learn the hard way that being a newcomer to the floral design business did not mean that I had to go into suppliers' showrooms and warehouses unaware and unarmed.

- I did learn the hard way that you need to equip yourself with the skills and tactics that make you a savvy price negotiator and buyer in the floral markets. This applies to all products!

- A buyer doesn't have to be taken in by smooth-talking salespeople, difficult terminology, or confusing pricing schemes.

- Much of the marketing you encounter is meant to lure you into spending lots of money while keeping you confused and embarrassed to ask questions.

- It gives the supplier the upper hand and keeps customers, particularly new customers, off balance and in a fog.

- The supplier comes across as the expert and you, the novice purchaser, as the uninformed.

But, I'm telling you, don't play their games!

Thirty-five years is a long time to learn the ropes of selling and purchasing floral or other products and merchandise.

With my help, you will be able to learn the lessons that I have gleaned over those years, lessons that propelled me to become a —world- renowned wreath designer and —successful Internet marketer.

MAJOR GIFT MARKETS IN THE UNITED STATES

AmericasMart | Merchandise Mart | 240 Peachtree Street | Atlanta, GA, 30303 | Phone Line: 404-749-4826 | Fax Line: 404-749-4826

Boston Gift Show | Los Angeles Convention Center | Kentia & South Halls | 1201 S. Figueroa Street | Los Angeles, CA, 90015 | Phone Line: 678-285-3976 | Fax Line: 404-749-4826

California Gift Show | Merchandise Mart | 240 Peachtree Street | Atlanta, GA, 30303 | Phone Line: 678-285-3976 | Toll Free: 800-318-2238

Chicago | The Merchandise Mart | 222 Merchandise Mart Plaza | Chicago, IL, 60654 | Phone Line: 312-464-0508 | Fax Line: 312-464-0346

Columbus | The Columbus Marketplace | 1999 West Belt Drive | Columbus, OH, 43228 | Phone/Fax: 614-850-8390

Dallas | World Trade Center | 2050 Stemmons Freeway | Dallas, TX, 75207 | Phone Line: 972-771-5040 or 800-245-3484 | Fax Line: 972-722-9064

Denver Colorado Showroom | Denver Merchandise Mart | Phone Line: 303-295-7455

Kansas City | Kansas Showroom | Overland Park | K C Merchandise Mart | Phone Line: 913-491-5119

Los Angeles | L A Mart | 1933 S Broadway | Los Angeles, CA, 90007 | Phone Line: 213-765-0253 | Fax Line: 213-765-0254

Las Vegas | World Market Center | 495 S Grand Central Pkwy | Las Vegas, NV, 89106-4555 | Office Telephone: 702-382-6670

Minnetonka, Minnesota | Green-Minn Gift Mart | Phone Line: 800-835-9455

New York | 7 W New York | 7 W 34th Street Suite 1023 | New York, NY, 10001 | Office Telephone: 212-725-3237 | Fax Line: 212-725-3241

Orlando Gift Show | Orange County Convention Center | West Concourse, Hall WD2 | 9800 International Drive | Orlando, FL 32819 | Phone Line: 628-285-3976

Seattle Gift Show |Washington State Convention Center | 800 Convention Place | Seattle, WA 98101-2350 | Office Telephone: 678-285-3976 | Toll Free: 1-800-318-2238, Ext. 4573

MAJOR TRADE SHOWS IN THE UNITED STATES

There are many trade shows in the United States today. ASD is the largest one, and we have already discussed it.

Actually, there are way too many to list here. So here are a couple of links that may lead you to the trade shows you're looking for:

http://www.tsnn.com/top-250-us-shows-list

http://www.vegasmeansbusiness.com/planning-tools/local-vendor- search/

If, after reading this book, you would like a list of wholesale sources, Ryan Reger has just released an excellent resource. It is an e-book titled _Real Wholesale Sources._ I highly recommend it!

1. **ASAP** – Abbreviation for "as soon as possible".

2. **Asset** – Items of value, especially what an organization owns.

3. **Bartering** – A type of transaction involving no money or cash, where one party provides one type of goods in exchange for another type of goods. Bartering can be carried out domestically or globally.

4. **Bill of Lading** – A written receipt given by a carrier for goods accepted for transportation.

5. **Chargeback** – When an issuing chargeback reverses a transaction, taking funds from a merchant and returning those funds to a customer.

6. **COD** – A payment term meaning cash is paid upon delivery.

7. **Contract** – An agreement between individuals or organizations. For a contract to be legally enforceable, there must be an offer, there must be an acceptance, and there must be some consideration (something given in return for something else, such as goods or services).

8. **Drop-shipper** – The manufacturer/distributor agrees to transfer customer orders directly to the consumer or an establishment like Amazon.

9. **E-commerce** – Buying and selling products over

electronic networks. More often, it applies to online retailing and online business.

10.   **EIN** – Issued by the IRS, this is an Employee Identification Number, also known as a Federal Tax Identification Number. If you have employees, you need one of these numbers.

11.   **FOB** – An abbreviation for Free on Board, indicating the place where the title or ownership passes from the seller to the buyer.

12.   **Inventory Turnover** – Number of times the average inventory has been sold during the year. Calculated by dividing the cost of goods sold by the average value of inventory.

13.   **Investment** – The investing of money or capital in order to gain profitable returns as interest, income, or appreciation in value.

14.   **JIT** – An abbreviation for Just in Time, referring to a scheduling system that minimizes inventory by having material arrive just as it is about to be put to use.

15.   **Letter of Credit** – A form of payment, used especially in international trade that transfers funds from the buyer's bank account to the seller's bank account. An Irrevocable Letter of Credit cannot be cancelled or revoked by the buyer as long as all documents are proper and approved by the bank, and the goods have been delivered to the specified place for shipment to the buyer.

16. **Liability** – In accounting, it is what a company owes. In law, it is an obligation to do or refrain from doing something, a duty that eventually must be performed, or an obligation to pay money.

17. **Liquidation** – A sale intended to dispose of all of a given product inventory with the intention of not replenishing supplies.

18. **Liquidator** – A company that purchases closeout products for the purpose of resale.

19. **Output** – The actual unit that is produced.

20. **Outsourcing** – When an outside specialist is contracted by an organization to perform non-core business.

21. **Opening Order** – A minimum order with a copy of a reseller's permit and tax ID.

22. **Profit** – The amount of money left over after all expenses are deducted from the revenue of the business.

23. **Purchase Order** – The form that documents the purchase agreement or contract.

24. **Re-orders** – Orders that may or may not require a minimum. They usually do not cost as much as an opening order amount.

25. **Reseller** – A company that purchases goods or services for the purpose of resale, not consumption. In web economics, a reseller may

also be a form of affiliate marketer.

26. **Retail Sales** – Sales made directly to the public, whether at a storefront, crafts fair, open studio, or as the result of a special order.

27. **ROI** – An abbreviation for Return on Investment.

28. **SEO** – An abbreviation for Search Engine Optimization.

29. **Single Source** – Where one supplier is either the only one available for a particular product or is the only supplier used even though others are available.

30. **Vendor** – Another term for a supplier or seller.

31. **Terms; Credit Card** – Add your entire purchase on a credit card before the purchase is shipped.

32. **Terms; Net 30** – Payment terms, balance due in 30 days.

33. **Terms; Net 45** – Payment terms, balance due in 45 days.

34. **Terms; Net 60** – Payment terms, balance due in 60 days.

35. **Terms; Net 90** – Payment terms, balance due in 90 days.

36. **Terms; Net 120** – Payment terms, balance due in 120 days.

37.   **_Terms; Christmas Dating_** – Balance due on or before December 10; this can be up to six months with a good payment history.

38.   **_Wholesale_** – Buyers purchase goods in bulk quantities from either manufacturers or importers, and then sell in smaller quantities to retail stores.

APPENDIX 2 – APPLY FOR A BUSINESS LICENSE

As we have discussed earlier in this book, there are many of you that do not have a business license. You may not have ever needed one, nor do you have a desire to get one now. All of the information about attending wholesale markets and trade shows is for those of you who do have a sales tax ID number.

I certainly think it is profitable for you in many ways to acquire your sales tax ID number and business license. For those of you interested in getting your own business license so you can purchase directly from the wholesale industry, please read on to see how simple that process is.

We have tracked down the business license requirements from every state in the USA and put them at your fingertips.

Just read the copy of the Small Business Administration (SBA) website page on the following pages and go to that website by **CLICKING HERE.**

Follow the instructions:

1. Enter your city and state or zip code.

2. Enter the general type of business you are in.

3. Proceed with the particular application steps for your location.

Again, that link to the website you need is gained by **CLICKING HERE**.

Following are links to several sites that may be of help in acquiring a business license:

http://www.sos.state.tx.us/corp/businessstructure.shtml

http://www.legalzoom.com/sitemap-dba-state-requirements1.html

http://dbafilingonline.com/dba-by-state/

OBTAIN BUSINESS LICENSES & PERMITS
FIND BUSINESS LICENSES & PERMITS

In order to operate your business, you must comply with a wide range of local, state, and federal rules. SBA's Business Licenses and Permits tool can help you navigate through this process.

Find Licenses and Permits for your Business

Go to the IRS site to enter your zip code in the box below, and select your business type to see which licenses and permits apply to your small business, along with links to web pages, application forms, and instructions.

If your type of business is not listed, select "General Licensing" and follow the links to your state and local licensing agencies to find licensing requirements for your specific business.

More Information about Business Licenses and Permits

Federal Licenses and Permits – For more detailed information on specific federal licenses that your business may need, refer to the Obtaining Business Licenses & Permits guide.

State Licenses and Permits – For state-specific licensing and permit information, select your state from the list below:

Alphabetical listing of states and territories with license and permit information.

- Alabama
- Alaska
- Arizona
- Arkansas
- California
- Colorado
- Connecticut
- Delaware
- District of
- Columbia
- Florida
- Georgia
- Guam
- Hawaii
- Idaho
- Illinois
- Indiana
- Iowa
- Kansas

- Kentucky
- Louisiana
- Maine
- Maryland
- Massachusetts
- Michigan
- Minnesota
- Mississippi
- Missouri
- Montana
- Nebraska
- Nevada
- New Hampshire
- New Jersey
- New Mexico
- New York
- North Carolina
- North Dakota

- Ohio
- Oklahoma
- Oregon
- Pennsylvania
- Puerto Rico
- Rhode Island
- South Carolina
- South Dakota
- Tennessee
- Texas
- U.S. Virgin Islands
- Utah
- Vermont
- Virginia
- Washington
- West Virginia
- Wisconsin
- Wyoming

Related Blogs:

- How to Find the Right License and Permit for Your New Business

- Run a Home-Based Business? – Find the Licenses and Permits You Need

- The Legal Steps Involved in Moving Your Business to a New State - FAQs Answered

APPENDIX 3 – APPLY FOR A SALES TAX NUMBER

TAXPAYER IDENTIFICATION NUMBERS (TIN)

A Taxpayer Identification Number (TIN) is an identification number used by the Internal Revenue Service (IRS) in the administration of tax laws. It is issued either by the Social Security Administration (SSA) or by the IRS. A Social Security number (SSN) is issued by the SSA, whereas all other TINs are issued by the IRS.

DO I NEED ONE?

A TIN must be furnished on returns, statements, and other tax-related documents. For example, a number must be furnished when filing your tax returns. A change in IRC section 6109 regulations in 1996 mandated the use of a TIN on tax returns.

HOW DO I GET A TIN?

The IRS expects the type of business (sole proprietorship, partnership, etc.) to be formed and filed with the state in which the business resides before applying for the Federal Employer Identification Number (FEIN) number. You also must submit evidence of your identity, age, and U.S. citizenship or lawful alien status.

The IRS has enhanced the speed of this process so that one can obtain a FEIN in a matter of minutes via the telephone at 1-800-829-4933 (from 7:00 a.m. until 10:00 p.m.) or the IRS website at **www.irs.gov/businesses/index.html**.

The necessary IRS Form to be completed is Form SS-4. These services are free. This form and its instructions can be viewed and printed via the IRS website. Also try the **Employer ID Numbers (FEIN)page**:
http://www.irs.gov/businesses/small/article/0,,id=98350,00.h tml

***My Secret Vendors*:** If you have enjoyed this book on sourcing products at markets and trade shows, you might also be interested in *"My Secret Vendors"*. Do you have a version of this yet? It has been updated five times, and each person received updates absolutely FREE!

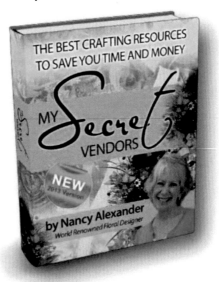

"My Secret Vendors" is my bestselling book on wreath-making supplies. Now, if you are a man, this may not interest you at all, but if you're a woman interested in arts and crafts as well as floral design, this could certainly be of value to you.

This downloadable e-book is over 450 pages long and gives you access to all of my secret and best vendors that I have used for a long time. If you want to make wreaths like mine, then you certainly can with the very same supplies. Find more information at: http://mysecretvendors.com/

Testimonial from a Happy Reader of *My Secret Vendors*:

No more hours of searching for the best vendors!

"I cannot describe what a help the "Secret Vendor List" has been for me! It has saved me money! It is so easy to sit down at my computer in the comfort of my own home. Browsing through websites of vendors, I am overcome with ideas for my next wreath and then the next as I look at their sites.

Nancy's taste is impeccable, so I don't worry at all when I order any of her suggestions online. After all, it was her taste which drew me to her in the first place. Thank you!" Beverly H.

Ladybug Wreaths Newsletter: Would you like to receive my free weekly newsletter containing decorating ideas, design tips, free how-to videos, or special deals? Visit:

http://www.LadybugWreaths.com.

Instructional DVDs and Videos: I offer over 20 instructional videos that show you step-by-step how to make different styles of wreaths, bows, arrangements, or centerpieces. To view the list of video offerings, go to:

http://ladybugwreaths.com/doorwreaths/product/dvds/
http://ladybugwreaths.com/doorwreaths/download-videos/

Workshops & Coaching: Private workshops and coaching are available upon request.

Nancy's Private Community – Best Of Nancy:

"Best of Nancy" is an all access private community site stocked with training and a very active forum. Our members are provided exclusive access to a private Facebook group, "Nancy Alexander, BestOfNancy.com".

Our community consists of a forum, video training, monthly updates, and bonuses. The forum is a great place to ask questions, meet other like-minded artisans, and find encouragement. The video training covers all the essential elements for selling your creations on the Internet.

http://www.BestOfNancy.com

Connect with Nancy on Facebook:

I have over 10,000 fans that follow me on Facebook, and I would love for you to be one of them! I do hope you will join us.

https://www.facebook.com/nancyladybugwreaths

Ladybug Wreaths Certified: Ladybug Certified is filled with supplies just like I use in my wreaths. There are wreath forms, greenery, mushrooms, moss, fresh rolls of honeysuckle vine, and flowers. You'll also find a huge selection of many different ribbons that I'm sure you'll love if you are into making your own wreaths!
http://www.LadybugCertified.com

How-To Books on Kindle: If you would like to download any of my Kindle books on wreath design or purchase one of my books on Amazon, they are available under Books: Author: Nancy Alexander.
http://ladybugwreaths.com/doorwreaths/nancysbooks

YouTube Videos: Learn to make a bow, a wreath, and so many other projects you'll love! I have more than 1.6 million views on these videos.
http://www.youtube.com/LadybugWreaths

"Every great dream begins with a dreamer. Always remember, you have within you the strength, the patience, and the passion to reach for the stars to change the world." - Harriet Tubman

Made in the USA
Lexington, KY
26 February 2018